NATIONAL GEOGRAPHIC KiDS

PUZZLE BOOK

UNDER THE SEA

Published by Collins
An imprint of HarperCollins Publishers
Westerhill Road
Bishopbriggs
Glasgow G64 2QT
www.harpercollins.co.uk

HarperCollins Publishers
1st Floor, Watermarque Building, Ringsend Road, Dublin 4, Ireland

In association with National Geographic Partners, LLC

NATIONAL GEOGRAPHIC and the Yellow Border Design are trademarks of the National Geographic Society, used under license.

First published 2019

ISBN 978-0-00-832151-2

10 9 8 7 6 5 4

If you would like to comment on any aspect of this book, please contact us at the above address or online.
natgeokidsbooks.co.uk
collins.reference@harpercollins.co.uk

Paper from responsible sources.

Acknowledgements

Cover images
Front – clown fish © Kitch Bain/Shutterstock.com; puffer fish © Eric Isselee/Shutterstock.com; orca © Mike Price/Shutterstock.com; dolphin © ArchMan/Shutterstock.com; Angelfish © Steven R Smith/Shutterstock.com; Star fish © pukach/Shutterstock.com Back – turtle © S hane Myers Photography/Shutterstock.com; coral © arka38/Shutterstock.com; mandarin fish © bluehand/Shutterstock.com; shark © Rich Carey/Shutterstock.com

Images in order of appearance
P2 © itor/Shutterstock.com; P3 © Kletr/Shutterstock.com; P7 © bluehand/Shutterstock.com; P8 © Steven R Smith/Shutterstock.com; P9(t) © Four Oaks/Shutterstock.com;(b) © Eric Isselee/Shutterstock.com; P10 © Kletr/Shutterstock.com; P11 © Rich Carey/Shutterstock.com; P12 © asawinimages/Shutterstock.com; P13 © bluehand/Shutterstock.com; P15(tl) © kelldallfall/Shutterstock.com; P15(tr) © orlandin/Shutterstock.com; P15(ml) © Daniel Huebner/Shutterstock.com; P15(mr) © Rich Carey/Shutterstock.com; P15(bl) © Leonardo Gonzalez/Shutterstock.com; P15(br) © Pavaphon Supanantananont/Shutterstock.com; P16(t) © Rich Carey/Shutterstock.com; P16(b) © Eric Isselee/Shutterstock.com; P17 © Kletr/Shutterstock.com; P18 © Tono Balaguer/Shutterstock.com; P19(t) © cynoclub/Shutterstock.com; P19(b) © Anna Azimi/Shutterstock.com; P21 © Eric Isselee/Shutterstock.com; P22 © Jeff Stamer/Shutterstock.com; P23 © Mike Price/Shutterstock.com; P24 © Ondrej Prosicky/Shutterstock.com; P25 © vklikov/Shutterstock.com; P26 © Joost van Uffelen/Shutterstock.com; P27 © wildestanimal/Shutterstock.com; P29(tl) © Chase Dekker/Shutterstock.com; P29(tr) © wildestanimal/Shutterstock.com; P29(ml) © Yann hubert/Shutterstock.com; P29(mr) © Tom Middleton/Shutterstock.com; P29(bl) © Vladimir Melnik/Shutterstock.com; P29(br)©Dmytro Pylypenko/Shutterstock.com; P30–31 ©Chase Dekker/Shutterstock.com; P32 © Tory Kallman/Shutterstock.com; P33(t) Neirfy/Shutterstock.com; P33(b) © svrid79/Shutterstock.com; P34 ©tryton2011/Shutterstock.com; P35 ©polarman/Shutterstock.com; P37 © wildestanimal/Shutterstock.com; P38 © Vicki L. Miller/Shutterstock.com; P39(t) © Martin Prochazkacz/Shutterstock.com; P39(b) Gilberto Villasana/Shutterstock.com; P40 © Grant M Henderson/Shutterstock.com; P41 © Laura Dinraths/Shutterstock.com; P42 © haveseen/Shutterstock.com; P43 © Dirk M. de Boer/Shutterstock.com; P45(tl) © stephan kerkhofs/Shutterstock.com; P45(tr) © Andrea Izzotti/Shutterstock.com; P45(ml) © Michael Bogner/Shutterstock.com P45(mr) © LuisMiguelEstevez/Shutterstock.com; P45(bl) © iamjeffery/Shutterstock.com; P45(br) © Andrea Izzotti/Shutterstock.com; P46 © Shane Gross/Shutterstock.com; P47 © Chainarong Phrammanee/Shutterstock.com; P48 © belizediversity/Shutterstock.com; P49(t) © frantisekhojdysz/Shutterstock.com; P49(b) © IrinaK/Shutterstock.com; P51 © Richard Whitcombe/Shutterstock.com; P52 © Eric Isselee/Shutterstock.com; P53 © Mati Nitibhon/Shutterstock.com; P54 © Andrey Starostin/Shutterstock.com; P55(t) © NaniP/Shutterstock.com; P55(b) © Chris Moody/Shutterstock.com; P56 © SChantra/Shutterstock.com; P57 © Ivan Kuzmin/Shutterstock.com; P59(tl) © bearacreative/Shutterstock.com; P59(tr) © zaferkizilkaya/Shutterstock.com; P59(ml) © kaschibo/Shutterstock.com; P59(mr) © e_rik/Shutterstock.com; P59(bl) © Alexius Sutandio/Shutterstock.com; P59(br) © Luke Suen/Shutterstock.com; P60 © NaniP/Shutterstock.com; P61(t) © Laura Dinraths/Shutterstock.com; P61(b) © Andrew Burgess/Shutterstock.com; P62 © Andaman/Shutterstock.com; P63(t) © ND700/Shutterstock.com; P63(b) © COZ/Shutterstock.com; P65 © Rich Carey/Shutterstock.com; P66 © Brendan Delzin/Shutterstock.com; P67(t) © Bunwit Unseree/Shutterstock.com; P67(b)By Aloaiza - Own work, CC BY 3.0. https://commons.wikimedia.org/w/index.php?curid=3582452; P68 By Rasmussen AR, Murphy JC, Ompi M, Gibbons JW, Uetz P (2011) - Rasmussen AR, Murphy JC, Ompi M, Gibbons JW, Uetz P (2011) Marine Reptiles. PLoS ONE 6(11): e27373. doi:10.1371/journal.pone.0027373, CC BY 2.5, https://commons.wikimedia.org/w/index.php?curid=26417019; P69(t) © Don Mammoser/Shutterstock.com; P69(b) © Prentiss/Shutterstock.com; P70 © You Touch Pix of EuToch/Shutterstock.com; P71 © S.Rohrlach/Shutterstock.com; P72–73 © Andrey Armyagov/Shutterstock.com; P74 © Rich Carey/Shutterstock.com; P75(t) © Chatchantharangsee/Shutterstock.com; P75(b) © Bunwit Unseree/Shutterstock.com; P76 © SW_Stock/Shutterstock.com; P77(t) © Rich Carey/Shutterstock.com; P77(b) © Kalaeva/Shutterstock.com; P79 © ChristianChan/Shutterstock.com; P80 © Laura Dinraths/Shutterstock.com; P81 © Marius Dobilas/Shutterstock.com; P82 © Martin Prochazkacz/Shutterstock.com; P83 © Joao Virissimo/Shutterstock.com; P84 © Levent Konuk/Shutterstock.com; P85 © Vladimir Wrangel/Shutterstock.com; P87(tl) © Richard Whitcombe/Shutterstock.com; P87(tr) © Damsea/Shutterstock.com; P87(ml) © David Litman/Shutterstock.com; P87(mr) © NatureDiver/Shutterstock.com; P87(bl) © Damsea/Shutterstock.com; P87(br) © Ethan Daniels/Shutterstock.com; P88 © IrinaK/Shutterstock.com; P89(t) © NaniP/Shutterstock.com; P89(b) © S.Rohrlach/Shutterstock.com; P90 © blue-sea.cz/Shutterstock.com; P91 © Dewald Kirsten/Shutterstock.com

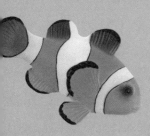

NATIONAL GEOGRAPHIC KiDS

PUZZLE BOOK

UNDER THE SEA

FACT-PACKED FUN

CONTENTS

FABULOUS FISH

MARVELLOUS MAMMALS

SUPER SHARKS AND RAYS

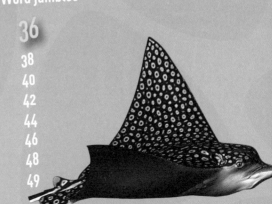

Fabulous fish

Dive into this chapter for fun facts and puzzles on our fishy friends.

MANDARIN FISH don't have scales like other fish! They have a **SLIMY SKIN** covered in **MUCUS** that has a **NASTY SMELL.**

CROSSWORDS

Help the angelfish crack the crosswords by solving the cryptic clues below.
Answers have the same amount of letters as the number in brackets.
Can you work out the fish keyword using the letters in the shaded squares?
See if you are right by flicking to page 92.

QUEEN ANGELFISH can live up to **15 YEARS** in the WILD!

Across

4   Marine animal with large tusks (6)
6   The end parts of the feet (4)
7   Block of chocolate; prevent (3)
8   Bluefin is a species of this fish (4)
9   Flat or level (4)
10 Small cake (3)
11 This must be paid before leaving a restaurant (4)
12 Whole; complete (6)

Down

1   Best-loved (9)
2   Likely to happen (8)
3   Place with rides and fun things to do (5,4)
5   Might; power (8)

The **GOLIATH GROUPER** can grow to at least **2.5 METRES (8 FT)** long.

A **PORCUPINE FISH** can **INFLATE** its body to about **THREE TIMES** its normal size.

Across

1. ___ energy: energy that comes from natural resources (9)
5. Letters that are not capital letters (5,4)
8. House made of solid snow (5)
9. This follows morning (9)
12. Book that lists synonyms for words (9)

Down

1. Unwilling to do something (9)
2. At this moment (3)
3. Noise made by a sheep (3)
4. Large animals with trunks (9)
6. Impressive bird of prey (5)
7. Comic entertainer in a circus (5)
10. Foot part (3)
11. Item used to move a rowing boat (3)

SUDOKUS

Solve the sudokus with the clownfish.
Fill in the blank squares so that numbers 1 to 6 appear once in each row,
column and 3 x 2 box. See if you are right by flicking to page 92.

	4	3			
		5	3	1	
	2		4		
		4		5	
	5	6	1		
				5	4

CLOWNFISH
are also known as
ANEMONEFISH!

Puzzle 1:

				2	4
	6		5		
3	2				5
1				4	3
		5		1	
2	1				

Puzzle 2:

	5				2
3	2				
	1	2			4
6			2	1	
				4	1
4				2	

Wordsearches

Triggerfish is on the lookout for her friends!
Search left to right, up and down to find the words listed in the boxes below.
See if you are right by flicking to page 92.

The **BANDED BUTTERFLY** fish always has a **STRIPE** covering its eye. This confuses **PREDATORS** as they can't tell which end of the body is the **HEAD** and which is the **TAIL**.

y	r	a	r	i	i	k	g	p	e
h	a	d	d	o	c	k	t	a	s
g	y	b	o	m	l	s	u	r	s
o	s	l	m	o	o	e	n	r	h
l	e	u	a	r	w	a	a	o	a
d	s	e	n	a	n	h	t	t	r
f	g	t	l	y	f	o	u	f	k
i	a	a	m	e	i	r	q	i	y
s	a	n	t	e	s	s	z	s	y
h	z	g	r	l	h	e	m	h	u

blue tang

clownfish

haddock

moray eel

parrotfish

ray

seahorse

shark

tuna

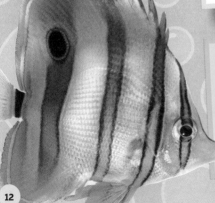

a	s	a	i	l	f	i	s	h	f
a	a	g	c	l	s	t	m	o	l
w	n	u	s	c	w	e	a	c	y
a	g	p	a	g	o	x	c	v	i
c	e	p	l	r	r	d	k	d	n
a	l	y	m	o	d	h	e	b	g
r	f	i	o	u	f	i	r	u	f
p	i	a	n	p	i	k	e	a	i
s	s	r	l	e	s	b	l	n	s
m	h	f	n	r	h	j	m	s	h

angelfish

carp

flying fish

grouper

guppy

mackerel

pike

sailfish

salmon

swordfish

A **TRIGGERFISH** can rotate each of its **EYEBALLS INDEPENDENTLY.**

CLOSE UP

Match the mind-boggling magnifications to the named pictures opposite. See if you are right by flicking to page 93.

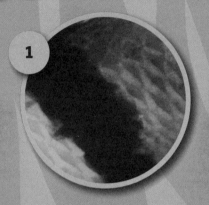
1

2

3

4

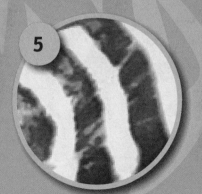
5

6

Sailfish
1

Yellowbanded pipefish
2

Flying fish
3

Moray eel
4

Bluehead wrasse
5

Parrotfish
6

MAZES

Lead the seahorse through the maze.
Work your way around the maze until you reach the exit.
See if you are right by flicking to page 93.

SEAHORSES suck up food through their **SNOUT** like a **VACUUM CLEANER!**

THE LONGHORN COWFISH is like a **LITTLE ARMOURED** tank! It's boxy body is covered in **SIX-SIDED** scales that are **FUSED** together.

The **LIONFISH** gets its name from its **LONG COLOURFUL SPINES** and **FINS** that resemble a **LION'S MANE**.

GUESS WHAT?

Can you guess the answers to the fish questions below?
Check your guesses by flicking to page 93.

1. The blue tang fish is also known as:
a) The dentist
b) The surgeon
c) The nurse

2. Where do clownfish live?
a) Anemones
b) Kelp forests
c) Rocky crevices

3. The fastest fish in the ocean is the:
a) Pufferfish
b) Sailfish
c) Cuttlefish

4. The goliath grouper can grow to at least:
a) 1 metre
b) 2 metres
c) 2.5 metres

5. The leafy seadragon can grow up to:
a) 25 cm
b) 50 cm
c) 100 cm

6. Groups of fish are called:
a) Hospitals
b) Houses
c) Schools

7. Fish use what to breathe?
a) Fins
b) Gills
c) Tail

8. A bluefin tuna can weigh up to:
a) 450 kg
b) 900 kg
c) 1,500 kg

9. Which fish has no tail?
a) Cloudfish
b) Moonfish
c) Sunfish

10. A parrotfish doesn't have what?
a) A stomach
b) A heart
c) A kidney

BLUEFIN TUNA has historically **WEIGHED** up to **900 KG** (2,000 lb) and reached **LENGTHS** of nearly 4 metres (13 ft).

WORD JUMBLES

Blue tang needs help to rearrange the jumbled letters to form the names of other fish. See if you are right by flicking to page 93.

E N I G H S F L A

R O G R U P E

L F N G H F S Y I I

BLUE TANG fish are both BLUE and YELLOW when they're young, but become totally BLUE when fully grown.

LEAFY SEADRAGONS are not good SWIMMERS! They FLOAT where the ocean current takes them.

T A N U

T G L B E A U N

Marvellous mammals

Explore this chapter for fun facts and puzzles about sea mammals.

In water, **SEA LIONS** can reach **SPEEDS** of **40 KM/HOUR** (25 miles/H).

CROSSWORDS

Help the manatee crack the crosswords by solving the cryptic clues below.
Answers have the same amount of letters as the number in brackets.
Can you work out the fish keyword using the letters in the shaded squares?
See if you are right by flicking to page 94.

MANATEES are related to **ELEPHANTS,** not dolphins or whales!

Across

1 Quick drawing (6)
6 Amuse (9)
7 The person who runs your school (4)
8 Container for flowers (4)
9 Hotel area (9)
11 Coronation ___ : soap opera (6)

Down

1 Person who looks after sheep (8)
2 Way in (8)
3 Road vehicle (3)
4 Publication bought at a newsagent (8)
5 Global computer network you use to visit websites (8)
10 Household animal (3)

Also known as **KILLER WHALES, ORCAS** are not actually whales, but the **LARGEST DOLPHIN** species.

Across

1 Hot-air ____ : type of aircraft (7)
6 Spider's trap (3)
8 Opposite of downwards (7)
9 In opposition to (7)
10 A coloured fluid used for writing (3)
11 Planet that is eighth from the Sun (7)

Down

2 Emergency vehicle (9)
3 A surgical procedure (9)
4 Hard to deal with (7)
5 Error (7)
7 Playground item that moves back and forth (5)

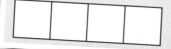

SUDOKUS

Solve the sudokus with the bearded seal.
Fill in the blank squares so that numbers 1 to 6 appear once in each row,
column and 3 x 2 box. See if you are right by flicking to page 94.

	3		5		
					6
2		1	3	5	
	5	3	1		2
5					
		4		1	

BEARDED SEALS get their name from the **WHITE WHISKERS** along their **SNOUTS** that look like a "beard".

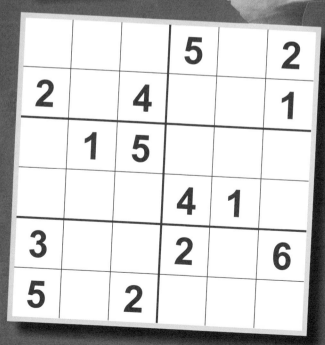

Wordsearches

Spotted dolphin is on the lookout for his friends.
Search left to right, up and down to find the words listed in the boxes below.
See if you are right by flicking to page 94.

Some adult
SPOTTED DOLPHINS
have so **MANY SPOTS**
they almost look
WHITE.

q	r	m	d	s	n	f	k	q	d
r	t	a	u	p	i	m	s	h	o
r	i	n	g	e	d	s	e	a	l
n	l	a	o	r	q	o	a	r	p
t	o	t	n	m	r	p	o	p	h
a	r	e	g	w	i	a	t	s	i
v	c	e	v	h	s	k	t	e	n
b	a	i	k	a	l	s	e	a	l
n	s	n	u	l	l	t	r	l	u
p	b	l	u	e	w	h	a	l	e

baikal seal
blue whale
dolphin
dugong
harp seal

manatee
orca
ringed seal
sea otter
sperm whale

s	p	o	l	a	r	b	e	a	r
m	i	n	k	e	w	h	a	l	e
o	a	j	b	w	a	l	r	u	s
n	t	f	i	n	w	h	a	l	e
k	s	m	q	e	m	t	r	x	i
s	e	a	l	i	o	n	r	o	w
e	v	a	q	u	i	t	a	b	h
a	p	o	r	p	o	i	s	e	a
l	b	o	n	a	r	w	h	a	l
l	p	a	t	r	t	a	a	w	e

SPERM WHALES have the **LARGEST BRAIN** of all animals, which can **WEIGH** up to **9 KILOGRAMMES!**

fin whale
minke whale
monk seal
narwhal
polar bear

porpoise
sea lion
sei whale
vaquita
walrus

CLOSE UP

Match the mind-boggling magnifications to the named pictures opposite. See if you are right by flicking to page 95.

1

2
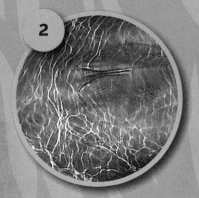

3

4

5

6

1 Blue whale

2 Narwhal

3 Humpback whale

4 Sea otter

5 Harp seal

6 Leopard seal

SPOT THE DIFFERENCE

Compare the two images of the whale.
Can you spot the five differences between the images?
See if you are right by flicking to page 95.

See if you are right by flicking to page 95.

HUMPBACK WHALES are known for **SINGING** loud, complex **"SONGS"** – lasting up to **30 MINUTES** long!

MAZES

Lead the beluga whale through the maze.
Work your way around the maze until you reach the exit.
See if you are right by flicking to page 95.

A **RISSO'S DOLPHIN** can go **UNDER WATER** for up to **30 MINUTES** without coming up for **AIR.**

The **BOTTLENOSE DOLPHIN** is one of the most **COMMONLY SEEN** dolphins in the **WORLD!**

BELUGA WHALES chirp, squeak, and whistle to each other so loudly, they're known as **"SEA CANARIES"!**

GUESS WHAT?

Can you guess the answers to the sea mammal questions below?
Check your guesses by flicking to page 95.

1. What sea mammal probably inspired mermaids?
   a) Dolphin
   b) Whale
   c) Dugong

2. Harp seal pups are what colour?
   a) White
   b) Grey
   c) Black

3. What is the biggest whale in the ocean?
   a) Sperm whale
   b) Narwhal
   c) Blue whale

4. Dolphins live in large groups called:
   a) Husks
   b) Pods
   c) Capsules

5. Walruses use what to find food on the ocean floor?
   a) Their whiskers
   b) Their tusks
   c) Their flippers

6. Sea otters use what tools to help them get into shellfish?
   a) Branches
   b) Rocks
   c) Shells

7. The southern elephant seal's trunk can be how long?
   a) 25 cm
   b) 50 cm
   c) 75 cm

8. The fastest dolphin in the ocean is the:
   a) Orca
   b) Spinner
   c) Bottlenose

9. Manatees are:
   a) Carnivores
   b) Omnivores
   c) Herbivores

10. How are sea mammals different from fish?
    a) They are warm blooded
    b) They breathe through lungs
    c) Both

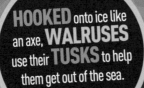

HOOKED onto ice like an axe, WALRUSES use their TUSKS to help them get out of the sea.

WORD JUMBLES

Ringed seal needs help to rearrange the jumbled letters
to form the names of other sea mammals.
See if you are right by flicking to page 95.

N G D G U O

R W H A N L A

E N T E A M A

A L S O I E N

M U C H W L A B E H K A P

RINGED SEALS
are one of the
SMALLEST
seal species.

Super Sharks and Rays

Watch out for fun facts and puzzles on sharks and rays in this chapter.

GREAT WHITE SHARKS can detect one drop of blood in **100 LITRES** of **WATER.**

CROSSWORDS

Help the stingray crack the crosswords by solving the cryptic clues below.
Answers have the same amount of letters as the number in brackets.
Can you work out the fish keyword using the letters in the shaded squares?
See if you are right by flicking to page 96.

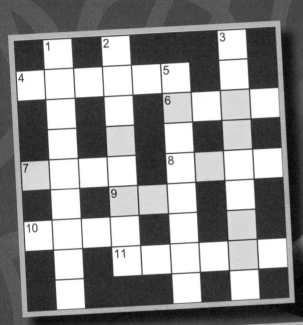

ANCIENT GREEK dentists used the **VENOM** from the stingray's spine as an **ANAESTHETIC.**

Across

4 Meal eaten outdoors (6)
6 Where you live (4)
7 Where you are right now (4)
8 Opposite of early (4)
9 Sum numbers together (3)
10 Opposite of more (4)
11 Number in a football team (6)

Down

1 Not the same (9)
2 Get bigger in size (8)
3 Occasionally or once in a while (9)
5 Kids (8)

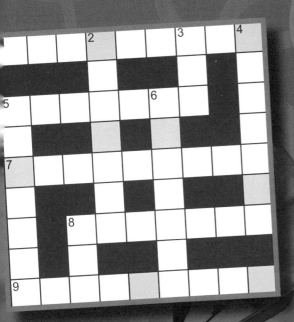

HAMMERHEAD sharks use their wide heads to **PIN STRINGRAYS** against the **SEA FLOOR.**

SHOVELNOSE guitarfish have the ability to **PUMP WATER** over their **GILLS,** allowing them to be perfectly **MOTIONLESS** on the sea floor.

Across

1 Ninth month (9)
5 Join together; link (7)
7 The person that lives next door to you (9)
8 Odd (7)
9 Crisis (9)

Down

2 This evening (7)
3 Small amount of something (3)
4 Move backwards (7)
5 Eat; use up a resource (7)
6 Green vegetable (7)
8 Understand; catch sight of (3)

SUDOKUS

Solve the sudokus with the basking shark.
Fill in the blank squares so that numbers 1 to 6 appear once in each row,
column and 3 x 2 box. See if you are right by flicking to page 96.

6					
1	4	5			3
	1				5
5				1	
4			6	3	2
					4

6				4	
			5		
		4	3	1	
	1	6	4		
		2			
	6				5

Unlike other rays, **ELECTRIC RAYS** don't have venomous scales or barbs. Instead they produce a strong **ELECTRIC DISCHARGE** from massive organs at the base of their **PECTORAL FINS.**

		4			
5	1				3
4			6		
		6			5
2				1	4
			5		

Wordsearches

The giant manta ray is on the lookout for his friends.
Search left to right, up and down to find the words listed in the boxes below.
See if you are right by flicking to page 96.

The **GIANT MANTA RAY** can measure up to **8 METRES (26 FT)** wide! This huge fish is **HARMLESS** however – unless you're plankton!

s	e	o	w	e	a	w	m	f	p
l	e	m	o	n	s	h	a	r	k
e	a	c	b	s	a	a	k	t	s
e	g	a	b	t	n	l	o	h	a
p	l	t	e	i	d	e	s	h	w
e	e	s	g	n	s	s	h	g	f
r	r	h	o	g	h	h	a	l	i
r	a	a	n	r	a	a	r	r	s
a	y	r	g	a	r	r	k	i	h
y	t	k	e	y	k	k	g	t	r

cat shark
eagle ray
lemon shark
mako shark
sand shark

sawfish
sleeper ray
stingray
whale shark
wobbegong

42

```
a  q  m  a  n  t  a  r  a  y
z  e  b  r  a  s  h  a  r  k
t  i  g  e  r  s  h  a  r  k
p  b  u  l  l  s  h  a  r  k
a  y  s  a  n  d  y  r  a  y
n  d  e  v  i  l  r  a  y  t
r  r  s  a  w  s  h  a  r  k
a  n  g  e  l  s  h  a  r  k
y  p  e  a  y  e  d  x  t  p
n  u  r  s  e  s  h  a  r  k
```

ZEBRA SHARKS have a **FLEXIBLE BODY** that allows them to **WRIGGLE** into **TIGHT SPACES** where small fish are often hiding.

angelshark
bull shark
devil ray
manta ray
nurse shark

panray
sandy ray
sawshark
tiger shark
zebra shark

CLOSE UP

Match the mind-boggling magnifications to the named pictures opposite. See if you are right by flicking to page 97.

1

2

3

4
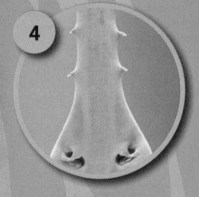

5

6
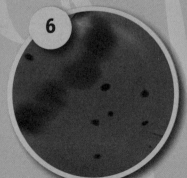

Porcupine ray

1

Sawfish

2

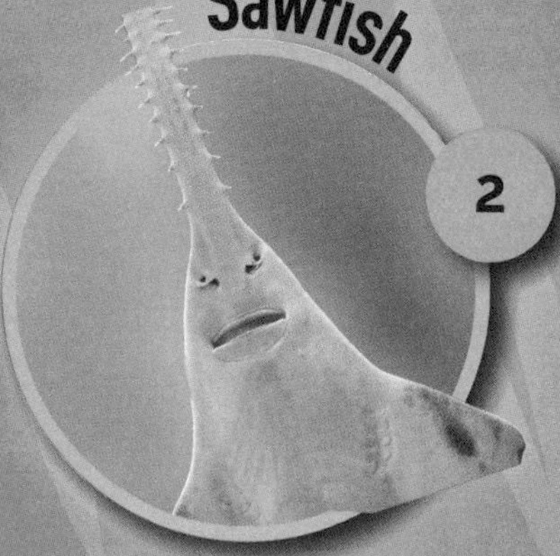

Lemon shark

3

Angelshark

4

Devil ray

5

Nurse shark

6

MAZES

Lead the tiger shark through the maze.
Work your way around the maze until you reach the exit.
See if you are right by flicking to page 97.

TIGER SHARKS will **EAT** anything, including **OTHER SHARKS,** licence plates and tyres!

GUESS WHAT?

Can you guess the answers to the shark and ray questions below?
Check your guesses by flicking to page 97.

1. How fast can a great white shark swim?
a) 55 km/h
b) 15 km/h
c) 80 km/h

2. The largest shark is the:
a) Tiger shark
b) Whale shark
c) Nurse shark

3. Baby sharks are called:
a) Cubs
b) Sharklings
c) Pups

4. A hammerhead shark uses its head to:
a) Swim backwards
b) Trap prey
c) Hammer nails

5. Shark skeletons are made of:
a) Cartilage
b) Bone
c) They don't have a skeleton

6. The giant manta ray can grow up to:
a) 8 metres
b) 10 metres
c) 12 metres

7. Electric rays do what to scare off predators?
a) Bite them
b) Sting them
c) Shock them

8. The devil ray can leap how high into the air?
a) 1.5 metres
b) 2 metres
c) 2.5 metres

9. The spotted eagle ray's pattern:
a) Is the same on every ray
b) Is unique like a fingerprint
c) Only appears on the young

10. A stingray's mouth is found on:
a) The underside of its body
b) The front of its head
c) The bottom of its tail

SPOTTED EAGLE RAYS have flat snouts that look like a **DUCK'S BILL.**

WORD JUMBLES

Spiny dogfish needs help to rearrange the jumbled letters to form the names of other sharks and rays.
See if you are right by flicking to page 97.

| Y | G | N | R | S | I | T | A |

| E | D | E | H | M | R | M | H | A | A |

| W | F | H | A | S | I | S |

| G | T | E | H | R | A | I | R | S | K |

| Y | T | A | M | A | R | A | N |

Schools of **SPINY DOGFISH** sharks **HUNT** down **SMALLER** fish in **DOG-LIKE PACKS!**

TASSELLED WOBBEGONG SHARKS perfectly blend into **CORAL REEFS** due to their **BLOTCHY COLOUR.**

Magnificent molluscs and shellfish

Discover fun facts and puzzles on molluscs and shellfish in this chapter.

The **PEACOCK MANTIS SHRIMP** has hammerlike claws that move as fast as **23 METRES PER SECOND (75 FT/SEC)** – a speed **50** times **FASTER** than a **BLINK** of a human **EYE!**

CROSSWORDS

Help the hermit crab crack the crosswords by solving the cryptic clues below.
Answers have the same amount of letters as the number in brackets.
Can you work out the fish keyword using the letters in the shaded squares?
See if you are right by flicking to page 98.

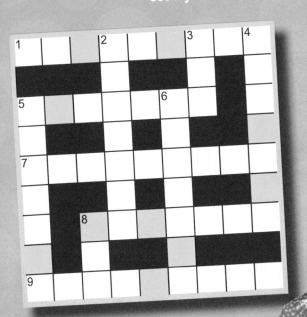

HERMIT CRABS have **SOFT UNPROTECTED** bodies. To protect themselves they use **OLD SHELLS AS ARMOUR.**

Across

1 Tennis tournament played on grass (9)
5 Container on wheels used in a supermarket (7)
7 Large fruit (9)
8 Common conjunction (7)
9 Bright flash that is followed by thunder (9)

Down

2 Feel sure a thing is true (7)
3 Not wet (3)
4 Not in any place (7)
5 Normal and usual (7)
6 Describe; make clear (7)
8 A small insect (3)

(6,4)

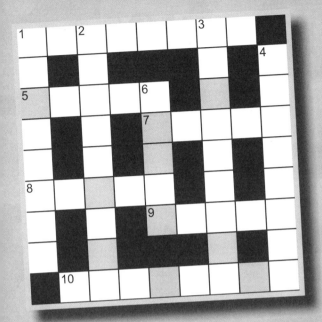

TIGER PRAWNS are **DECAPODS**, which means they have **TEN LEGS!**

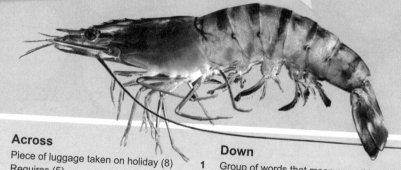

Across

1 Piece of luggage taken on holiday (8)
5 Requires (5)
7 Birds flap these in order to fly (5)
8 Sound (5)
9 Part of the hand (5)
10 Difficult to walk on without falling over (8)

Down

1 Group of words that mean something (8)
2 The same as something else (9)
3 Your way of writing your name (9)
4 Time when the whole school gets together (8)
6 Sugary (5)

(5,5)

SUDOKUS

Solve the sudokus with the lobster.
Fill in the blank squares so that numbers 1 to 6 appear once in each row,
column and 3 x 2 box. See if you are right by flicking to page 98.

	5	3			
				1	
2					
			5		3
3		5			
		4			6
			2	5	

The
GIANT PACIFIC OCTOPUS is known to use **TOOLS** and recognise different **HUMANS!**

The **HUMBOLDT SQUID** lives a short and fierce life. This big squid can be **LONGER** than a **PERSON** and **LIVES** only about **ONE YEAR** – possibly two.

Top puzzle:

	6			1	5
				4	6
2	4				
				4	1
	5	3			
	2	4			1

Bottom puzzle:

2	4		3		
		3	2		
				5	4
4	5				
	1		3		
	2			6	1

Wordsearches

The ghost crab is on the lookout for its friends. Search left to right, up and down to find the words listed in the boxes below.
See if you are right by flicking to page 98.

d	s	c	a	m	p	i	h	t	f
t	a	r	w	c	p	p	e	i	g
s	c	a	l	l	o	p	r	g	e
h	q	y	f	k	r	s	m	e	o
u	u	f	a	v	p	q	i	r	d
k	r	i	l	l	p	u	t	p	u
a	i	s	i	c	r	i	c	r	c
s	t	h	h	f	q	d	r	a	k
l	o	b	s	t	e	r	a	w	p
y	o	y	s	t	e	r	b	n	o

crayfish
geoduck
hermit crab
krill
lobster

oyster
scallop
squid
tiger prawn

```
r b o c t o p u s e
b n g u a m l w h g
a a h t e b a i r i
r u o t m a n n i a
n t s l u i d k m n
a i t e s g c l p t
c l c f s h r e v c
l o r i e i a q a l
e i a s l a b q c a
w d b h p p f l l m
```

GHOST CRABS are so perfectly **CAMOUFLAGED** they're nearly **INVISIBLE** on the **SANDY BEACHES** where they live.

The **BLUE-RINGED OCTOPUS** is **SMALL** – its body is about the **SIZE** of a golf ball, and its arms are about **7 CM (2.8 INCHES)** long.

barnacle
cuttlefish
ghost crab
giant clam
land crab

mussel
nautiloid
octopus
shrimp
winkle

CLOSE UP

Match the mind-boggling magnifications to the named pictures opposite. See if you are right by flicking to page 99.

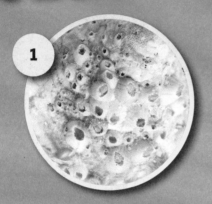

1

2

3

4

5

6

Flamingo tongue

1

Giant triton

2

Veined octopus

3

Acorn barnacle

4

Striped pyjama squid

5

Mimic octopus

6

MAZES

Lead the Japanese spider crab through the maze.
Work your way around the maze until you reach the exit.
See if you are right by flicking to page 99.

JAPANESE SPIDER CRABS
have legs that can span
4 METRES (13 FT)
across and they **WEIGH**
around **18 KG** (40 lb).

When a **SPANISH DANCER** slug feels threatened, it will **VIOLENTLY** flap its external gills and display its bright **WARNING COLOURS.** This reminded scientists of a **SPANISH FLAMENCO DANCER,** where it gets its name.

HORSESHOE CRABS have been around for at least **450 MILLION** years, making them one of the **OLDEST** living animals today!

GUESS WHAT?

Can you guess the answers to the mollusc and shellfish questions below?
Check your guesses by flicking to page 99.

1. Which one of these is a cephalopod?
   a) Shark
   b) Octopus
   c) Clownfish

2. How many arms does an octopus have?
   a) 10
   b) 8
   c) 5

3. How long have horseshoe crabs been around for?
   a) 150 million years
   b) 300 million years
   c) 450 million years

4. The spanish dancer slug looks like it is doing which dance?
   a) Flamenco
   b) Foxtrot
   c) Tango

5. A giant clam produces which precious item?
   a) Diamond
   b) Ruby
   c) Pearl

6. The veined octopus is also know as the:
   a) Coconut Octopus
   b) Pineapple Octopus
   c) Mango Octopus

7. The colour of lobster blood is:
   a) Red
   b) Blue
   c) Orange

8. Why won't you see peacock mantis shrimp in an aquarium?
   a) Their punch can crack the glass
   b) They're too hard to find in the sea
   c) They don't like living with other fish

9. How big does the striped pyjama squid grow?
   a) 7 metres
   b) 7 inches
   c) 7 centimetres

10. How wide can Japanese spider crabs' legs spread?
    a) 2 metres
    b) 4 metres
    c) 6 metres

WORD JUMBLES

Giant clam needs help to rearrange the jumbled letters to form the names of other molluscs and shellfish.
See if you are right by flicking to page 99.

U K G D O C E

O B H R S G T C A

I R P R O E M S M H R P E

U T C O P S O

E T B R O L S

The **GEODUCK,** pronouced "**GOOEY DUCK**" is a large clam native to North America.

You can often find **EMPEROR SHRIMP** on the back of **SEA CUCUMBERS.** This **PROTECTS** them from **PREDATORS** and they can feed off of parasites that live on the **SEA CUCUMBERS' SKIN.**

A **GIANT CLAM** produced the largest known pearl, which **WEIGHED 6.4 KG** (14 lb).

Riveting reptiles

Take a look around this chapter for fun facts and puzzles on turtles and other reptiles.

The **HAWKSBILL TURTLE** gets its **NAME** due to its **HOOKED SNOUT**.

CROSSWORDS

Help the turtle crack the crosswords by solving the cryptic clues below.
Answers have the same amount of letters as the number in brackets.
Can you work out the fish keyword using the letters in the shaded squares?
See if you are right by flicking to page 100.

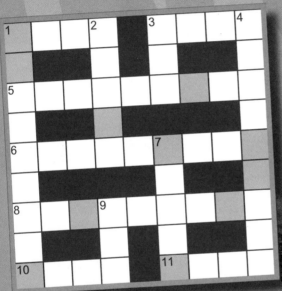

Unlike other turtles, the **LEATHERBACK TURTLE** does not have a **HARD SHELL!** It has small, bony plates covered by tough, **LEATHERY SKIN.**

Across

1. People sleep in these (4)
3. Additionally (4)
5. Flying vehicle (9)
6. Device used to study stars and planets (9)
8. Period of two weeks (9)
10. Type of light (4)
11. Mars (anag.) (4)

Down

1. Very attractive (9)
2. Said something (5)
3. The whole of (3)
4. These are made from beaten eggs cooked in frying pans (9)
7. Country in Asia whose capital is Beijing (5)
9. Opposite of bottom (3)

The **WORLD'S LARGEST REPTILE** is the **SALTWATER CROCODILE.** Males can grow to be **5 METRES (17 FT) LONG.**

Across

1. Leave a place (6)
6. Yellow vegetable (9)
7. Opposite of home (4)
8. Cone (anag.) (4)
9. Hot ____ : sweet cocoa drink (9)
11. Mars or Jupiter, for instance (6)

Down

1. Length of space between two points (8)
2. Animal that hunts others (8)
3. Rodent with a long tail (3)
4. Very high hill (8)
5. Excite the curiosity of someone (8)
10. Bird of prey (3)

The **YELLOW-BELLIED SEA SNAKE** is the most widely ranging snake in the world and is completely aquatic. Because it never needs to come to land it may be found far out in **OPEN TROPICAL OCEANS.**

SUDOKUS

Solve the sudokus with the sea snake. Fill in the blank squares so that numbers 1 to 6 appear once in each row, column and 3 x 2 box. See if you are right by flicking to page 100.

4	5			6	
		2			5
		1			4
2			1		
6			5		
	2			1	6

BELCHER'S SEA SNAKE is one of the most **VENOMOUS SNAKES** in the **WORLD.** However, it is very timid and only **BITES** if it is being **MISTREATED.** It breathes air, and has valves over its nostrils that close underwater. It can hold its **BREATH** for as long as **7 TO 8 HOURS.**

4				5	2
			1		
3		2		6	
	4		5		3
		4			
6	1				5

MARINE IGUANAS SNEEZE frequently to expel **SALT** from glands near their **NOSES.**

FEMALE LOGGERHEAD TURTLES in the Pacific Ocean **MIGRATE** about **12,000 KM (7,500 MILES)** from **MEXICO'S** coast to lay their eggs on beaches in **JAPAN.**

				5	
	5			1	6
		1		3	5
5	3		6		
1	4			6	
	2				

Wordsearches

The olive sea snake is on the lookout for her friends.
Search left to right, up and down to find the words listed in the boxes below.
See if you are right by flicking to page 100.

c	r	o	c	o	d	i	l	e	q
s	g	l	g	p	a	a	o	k	m
h	r	a	a	o	w	s	g	e	r
e	e	t	l	t	k	t	g	d	e
l	e	b	a	t	s	e	e	t	p
l	n	a	p	e	b	r	r	u	t
n	z	c	a	d	i	n	h	r	i
g	d	k	g	r	l	b	e	t	l
o	s	a	o	s	l	o	a	l	e
t	s	s	s	f	y	x	d	e	x

The **KEMP'S RIDLEY SEA** turtle is the most **ENDANGERED** sea turtle in the world. They are also the **SMALLEST** sea turtle coming in at under **60 CM** on average and **WEIGHING** about **45 KG** once fully grown.

crocodile
flatback
galapagos
green
hawksbill

loggerhead
reptile
shell
turtle

a n a c o n d a a b
a c l o l i v e a e
s o i p a n d a a l
l r a y s c a l z c
i a a t c a v a a h
t l k h a a e a k e
h r e o l a n n e r
e e s n e a o a a s
r e a a s a m s r a
b f s e a s n a k e

OLIVE SEA SNAKES can grow over **2 METRES** (6 ft) **LONG.** They spend their full life-cycle in the ocean and have a flattened, **PADDLE**-like **TAIL** to help them **SWIM.**

anaconda
belchers
coral reef
olive

python
scales
sea snake
slither
venom

SPOT THE DIFFERENCE

Compare the two images of the sea.
Can you spot the five differences between the images?
See if you are right by flicking to page 101.

See if you are right by flicking to page 101.

Just like your bones, a **TURTLE'S SHELL** is actually part of its skeleton. It's made up of over **50 BONES** which include the turtle's **RIB CAGE** and **SPINE.**

MAZES

Lead the green turtle through the maze.
Work your way around the maze until you reach the exit.
See if you are right by flicking to page 101.

GREEN TURTLES are named for the **GREENISH COLOUR** of their fat and cartilage, not the colour of their shell, which is normally **BROWN OR OLIVE.**

OLIVE RIDLEY turtles are famous for **CLIMBING ASHORE** by the thousands to nest at the same time on the same beach. These group nestings are called **ARRIBADAS**, which is Spanish for **"ARRIVAL BY SEA"**.

SALTWATER CROCODILES have **STRONG, POWERFUL,** locking **JAWS** that they use to capture their **PREY**. Once caught, it is nearly impossible to escape its **DEADLY GRIP**.

GUESS WHAT?

Can you guess the answers to the turtle and reptile questions below?
Check your guesses by flicking to page 101.

1. How deep can a leatherback turtle dive?
   a) 800 metres
   b) 1,000 metres
   c) 1,500 meters

2. Where do turtles lay their eggs?
   a) The beach
   b) The ocean floor
   c) In rock pools

3. Babies that hatch from an egg are known as?
   a) Hatchlings
   b) Puppies
   c) Calves

4. On average how many eggs do sea turtles lay at a time?
   a) 10–30
   b) 50–80
   c) 100–120

5. The smallest sea turtle is the:
   a) Leatherback
   b) Kemp's Ridley
   c) Loggerhead

6. The saltwater crocodile can grow to be how long?
   a) 3 metres
   b) 5 metres
   c) 7 metres

7. The marine iguana is the only lizard known to:
   a) Have warm blood
   b) Hunt at night
   c) Swim and feed in the ocean

8. Which snake never needs to come onto land?
   a) Yellow-bellied sea snake
   b) Ornate reef sea snake
   c) Belcher's sea snake

9. There are around how many species of sea snake?
   a) 40
   b) 60
   c) 80

10. Turtle eggs look like what?
    a) Tennis balls
    b) Squash balls
    c) Ping-pong balls

Many **REPTILES** that **LIVE** in the **WATER** come back to **LAND** to lay their eggs. When the eggs **HATCH**, baby hatchlings must make their way back to the sea. Sea turtle **HATCHLINGS** use the glow of the **MOONLIGHT** on the water to guide them there.

WORD JUMBLES

Banded sea krait needs help to rearrange the jumbled letters to form the names of other turtles and reptiles. See if you are right by flicking to page 101.

L H W S B L I A K

E W S T L T R A A

B H L A E R C K A T E

R I O C L O C D E

N A S S K E A E

SEA TURTLES lay on average **110 EGGS**, which they **BURY** on the **BEACH.** Their eggs have a soft shell and are around the size of a **PING-PONG BALL!**

The **BANDED SEA KRAIT** is a **SEA SNAKE** that lives on coral reefs in the Indian and western Pacific oceans. They come ashore to **LAY EGGS,** drink freshwater, rest on rocks and **SHED THEIR SKIN.**

Cool corals and invertebrates

Delve into this chapter for fun facts and puzzles on corals and invertebrates.

SEA CUCUMBERS will EJECT their GUTS to SCARE AWARE PREDATORS!

CROSSWORDS

Help the jellyfish crack the crosswords by solving the cryptic clues below. Answers have the same amount of letters as the number in brackets. Can you work out the fish keyword using the letters in the shaded squares? See if you are right by flicking to page 102.

Unlike most **JELLYFISH**, the upside-down jellyfish **RARELY SWIMS!** It lies on the seafloor with its tentacles **FACING UPWARDS.**

Across
4 Container for a drink (3)
6 Strange; rare (7)
7 A building in which plays are performed (7)
8 Small balls of coloured glass used as toys (7)
10 Complete lack of sound (7)
11 Enquire (3)

Down
1 Country where one finds Sydney (9)
2 Sixth month (4)
3 Attractive insect with colourful wings (9)
4 Hint (4)
5 A person or company that issues books for sale (9)
8 Covering for the face (4)
9 Narrow road (4)

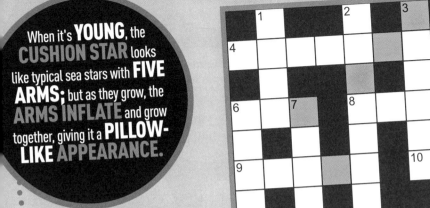

When it's **YOUNG**, the **CUSHION STAR** looks like typical sea stars with **FIVE ARMS;** but as they grow, the **ARMS INFLATE** and grow together, giving it a **PILLOW-LIKE APPEARANCE.**

Across

4 Device used by people who jump out of aircraft (9)
6 Small social insect (3)
8 What an active volcano might do (5)
9 Have faith in (5)
10 A long period of time (3)
12 Place in a school where lessons are taught (9)

Down

1 Chief in importance (4)
2 Einstein or Currie, for instance (9)
3 Time that has not yet happened (6)
5 Additional (5)
6 Room inside the roof of a house (5)
7 Bird with a big and brightly coloured beak (6)
11 Underground plant part (4)

SUDOKUS

Solve the sudokus with the jellyfish.
Fill in the blank squares so that numbers 1 to 6 appear once in each row,
column and 3 x 2 box. See if you are right by flicking to page 102.

The **LION'S MANE JELLYFISH** has hundreds of **TENTACLES** which can grow to be more than **30 METRES (100 FT)** long. Each tentacle contains stinging cells that work like **MINIATURE HARPOONS.**

	5	3			6
	6	1			
		5		2	
	4		6		
			4	3	
1			5	6	

Grid 1

	6		2		3
2				4	6
3					
					1
6	1				5
5		3		1	

Grid 2

		2	3		
6			2		
	6	5			4
1			6	3	
		6			2
		1	4		

Wordsearches

The moon jellyfish is on the lookout for his friends. Search left to right, up and down to find the words listed in the boxes below. See if you are right by flicking to page 102.

```
g  z  p  j  t  a  b  s  b  e
i  t  l  s  a  a  r  o  l  a
a  r  w  e  b  n  a  f  a  s
n  s  c  a  l  e  i  t  c  p
t  e  r  u  e  m  n  c  k  o
k  a  i  r  c  o  c  o  c  n
e  s  n  c  o  n  o  r  o  g
l  t  o  h  r  e  r  a  r  e
p  a  i  i  a  p  a  l  a  t
x  r  d  n  l  s  l  n  l  k
```

NUDIBRANCHS are a type of sea slug, known for their **MAGNIFICENT COLOURS.** There are ov **3,000 SPECIES** with more still being discovered

anemone	sea star
black coral	sea urchin
brain coral	soft coral
crinoid	sponge
giant kelp	table coral

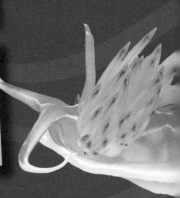

s	c	s	u	u	r	k	s	n	s
e	o	t	b	a	e	f	e	u	a
a	r	a	l	a	d	d	a	d	n
p	a	r	u	a	c	u	s	i	n
e	l	f	e	j	o	l	p	b	e
n	r	i	c	h	r	i	i	r	l
m	e	s	o	c	a	t	d	a	i
u	e	h	r	k	l	e	e	n	d
o	f	s	a	l	p	x	r	c	p
j	e	l	l	y	f	i	s	h	t

MOON JELLYFISH are found in coastal areas of the **NORTH ATLANTIC OCEAN**. They aren't very good at swimming and can be **STRANDED** on beaches after **STORMS** and **HIGH TIDES.**

annelid

blue coral

coral reef

jellyfish

nudibranch

red coral

salp

sea pen

sea spider

starfish

CLOSE UP

Match the mind-boggling magnifications to the named pictures opposite. See if you are right by flicking to page 103.

1 Crown of thorns starfish

2 Branching vase sponge

3 Purple-striped jellyfish

4 Sunflower star

5 Grooved brain coral

6 Staghorn coral

MAZES

Lead the Portuguese man o'war through the maze. Work your way around the maze until you reach the exit.
See if you are right by flicking to page 103.

The **PORTUGUESE MAN O' WAR** isn't actually a **JELLYFISH** but it is related to them. Each one is a colony of **IDENTICAL** individuals with different jobs, all working **TOGETHER** and **DEPENDENT** on each other.

The **MOUTH** of the
SEA ANEMONE is
also their **BOTTOM!**

The **BLUE GLAUCUS**
defends itself using
POISONOUS
CHEMICALS and stinging
cells **COLLECTED** from its
PREY.

GUESS WHAT?

Can you guess the answers to the coral and invertebrate questions below?
Check your guesses by flicking to page 103.

1. Where is the world's largest coral reef found?
   a) Chile
   b) Japan
   c) Australia

2. What tropical fish live in sea anemones?
   a) Clownfish
   b) Magicianfish
   c) Builderfish

3. How high can giant sea kelp grow?
   a) 15 metres
   b) 30 metres
   c) 45 metres

4. Coral bleaching happens when:
   a) Water gets too warm
   b) Fish eat the coral
   c) Corals get no sunlight

5. What is the world's largest sea star?
   a) Cushion sea star
   b) Crown of thorns star
   c) Sunflower star

6. Nudibranchs are types of:
   a) Fish
   b) Sea slugs
   c) Turtles

7. Jellyfish are found in:
   a) Indian and Pacific oceans
   b) Atlantic ocean
   c) Every ocean

8. Sea cucumbers have thousands of tubed:
   a) Feet
   b) Fingers
   c) Eyes

9. What happens when a sea star loses an arm?
   a) It changes colour
   b) It grows a new arm
   c) It dies

10. What invertebrates are almost all skeleton?
    a) Mud dollars
    b) Sand dollars
    c) Grass dollars

WORD JUMBLES

Box jellyfish needs help to rearrange the jumbled letters to form the names of other corals and invertebrates.
See if you are right by flicking to page 103.

F Y I E H L S L J

M A E U E R C S U C B

E M E A O N N

R A O C L

I R S F A S H T

The **BOX JELLYFISH** is the most TOXIC ANIMAL on Earth!

The **GRANULATED SEA STAR** has PLUMP ARMS that make it look like a **RUBBER GLOVE FILLED** with water. Its funny shape has earned it another common name: **DOUGHBOY STAR.**

91

Solutions

Page 8–9

Crosswords

	F	P				T		
W	A	L	R	U	S	H		
	V	O		T	O	E	S	
	O		B	A	R	M		
T	U	N	A		E	V	E	N
	R		B	U	N		P	
B	I	L	L		G		A	
	T		E	N	T	I	R	E
	E			H			K	

Keyword: ANGELFISH

R	E	N	E	W	A	B	L	E
E		O			A		L	
L	O	W	E	R	C	A	S	E
U		A		L			P	
C		I	G	L	O	O		
T		L		W			H	
A	F	T	E	R	N	O	O	N
N		O			A		T	
T	H	E	S	A	U	R	U	S

Keyword: GROUPER

Page 10–11

Sudokus

1	4	3	6	2	5
2	6	5	3	1	4
5	2	1	4	6	3
6	3	4	2	5	1
4	5	6	1	3	2
3	1	2	5	4	6

5	3	1	6	2	4
4	6	2	5	3	1
3	2	4	1	6	5
1	5	6	2	4	3
6	4	5	3	1	2
2	1	3	4	5	6

1	5	6	4	3	2
3	2	4	1	5	6
5	1	2	3	6	4
6	4	3	2	1	5
2	3	5	6	4	1
4	6	1	5	2	3

Page 12–13

Wordsearches

Close up

1 – 5 Bluehead wrasse

2 – 3 Flying fish

3 – 6 Parrotfish

4 – 1 Sailfish

5 – 2 Yellowbanded pipefish

6 – 4 Moray eel

Mazes

Guess what?

1. b) The surgeon

6. c) Schools

2. a) Anemones

7. b) Gills

3. b) Sailfish

8. b) 900 kg

4. c) 2.5 metres

9. c) Sunfish

5. a) 25 cm

10. a) Stomach

Word jumbles

ANGELFISH

GROUPER

FLYING FISH

TUNA

BLUE TANG

Solutions

Page 22–23
Crosswords

Crossword 1 grid:

```
S K E T C H
H   N   A   M       I
E N T E R T A I N
P   R   G       T
H E A D   V A S E
E   N       Z   R
R E C E P T I O N
D   E   E   N   E
    S T R E E T
```

Keyword: MANATEE

Crossword 2 grid:

```
  B A L L O O N
A   M       P   M
W E B   S   E   I
K   U P W A R D S
W   L   I   A   T
A G A I N S T   A
R   N   G   I N K
D   C       O   E
  N E P T U N E
```

Keyword: ORCA

Page 24–25
Sudokus

Sudoku 1:

6	3	2	5	4	1
1	4	5	2	3	6
2	6	1	3	5	4
4	5	3	1	6	2
5	1	6	4	2	3
3	2	4	6	1	5

Sudoku 2:

4	6	3	5	2	1
1	5	2	4	6	3
2	1	5	3	4	6
6	3	4	2	1	5
5	4	1	6	3	2
3	2	6	1	5	4

Sudoku 3:

1	3	6	5	4	2
2	5	4	3	6	1
4	1	5	6	2	3
6	2	3	4	1	5
3	4	1	2	5	6
5	6	2	1	3	4

Page 26–27
Wordsearches

Wordsearch 1:

```
q r m d s n f k q d
r t a u p i m s h o
r i n g e d s e a l
n l a o r q o a r p
t o t n m r p o p h
a r e g w i a t s i
v c e v h s k t e n
b a i k a l s e a l
n s n u l l t r l u
p b l u e w h a l e
```

Wordsearch 2:

```
s p o l a r b e a r
m i n k e w h a l e
o a j b w a l r u s
n t f i n w h a l e
k s m q e m t r x i
s e a l i o n r o w
e v a q u i t a b h
a p o r p o i s e a
l b o n a r w h a l
l p a t r t a a w e
```

Page 28–29 — Close up

1 – 4 Sea otter   2 – 1 Blue whale   3 – 2 Narwhal

4 – 5 Harp seal   5 – 6 Leopard seal   6 – 3 Humpback whale

Page 30–31 — Spot the difference

Page 32–33 — Mazes

Page 34–35 — Guess what?

1. c) Dugong
2. a) White
3. c) Blue whale
4. b) Pods
5. a) Their whiskers

6. b) Rocks
7. b) 50 cm
8. a) Orca
9. c) Herbivores
10. c) Both

Word jumbles

DUGONG   NARWHAL   MANATEE

SEA LION   HUMPBACK WHALE

Solutions

Page 38–39

Crosswords

	D	I			S			
P	I	C	N	I	C			
	F	C		H	O	M	E	
	F	R		I		E		
H	E	R	E		L	A	T	E
	R		A	D	D		I	
L	E	S	S		R		M	
	N		E	L	E	V	E	N
	T				N		S	

Keyword: HAMMERHEAD

S	E	P	T	E	M	B	E	R
			O			I		E
C	O	N	N	E	C	T		V
O			I		A			E
N	E	I	G	H	B	O	U	R
S			H		B			S
U		S	T	R	A	N	G	E
M		E			G			
E	M	E	R	G	E	N	C	Y

Keyword: STRINGRAY

Page 40–41

Sudokus

6	3	2	5	4	1
1	4	5	2	6	3
3	1	6	4	2	5
5	2	4	3	1	6
4	5	1	6	3	2
2	6	3	1	5	4

6	3	5	2	4	1
2	4	1	5	6	3
5	2	4	3	1	6
3	1	6	4	5	2
1	5	2	6	3	4
4	6	3	1	2	5

6	3	4	2	5	1
5	1	2	4	6	3
4	5	1	6	3	2
3	2	6	1	4	5
2	6	5	3	1	4
1	4	3	5	2	6

Page 42–43

Wordsearches

s	e	o	w	e	a	w	m	f	p
l	e	m	o	n	s	h	a	r	k
e	a	c	b	s	a	a	k	t	s
e	g	a	b	t	n	l	o	h	a
p	l	t	e	i	d	e	s	h	w
e	e	s	g	n	s	s	h	g	f
r	r	h	o	g	h	h	a	l	i
r	a	a	n	r	a	a	r	r	s
a	y	r	g	a	r	r	k	i	h
y	t	k	e	y	k	k	g	t	r

a	q	m	a	n	t	a	r	a	y
z	e	b	r	a	s	h	a	r	k
t	i	g	e	r	s	h	a	r	k
p	b	u	l	l	s	h	a	r	k
a	y	s	a	n	d	y	r	a	y
n	d	e	v	i	l	r	a	y	t
r	r	s	a	w	s	h	a	r	k
a	n	g	e	l	s	h	a	r	k
y	p	e	a	y	e	d	x	t	p
n	u	r	s	e	s	h	a	r	k

96

Page 44-45

Close up

1 – 4 Angelshark

2 – 3 Lemon shark

3 – 1 Porcupine ray

4 – 2 Sawfish

5 – 6 Nurse shark

6 – 5 Devil ray

Page 46-47

Mazes

Page 48-49

Guess what?

1. a) 55 km/h

2. b) Whale shark

3. c) Pups

4. b) Trap prey

5. a) Cartilage

6. a) 8 metres

7. c) Shock them

8. b) 2 metres

9. b) Is unique like a fingerprint

10. a) The underside of its body

Word jumbles

STINGRAY

HAMMERHEAD

SAWFISH

TIGER SHARK

MANTA RAY

Solutions

Crosswords

Crossword 1:
```
W I M B L E D O N
    E       R   O
T R O L L E Y     W
Y     I     X     H
P I N E A P P L E
I     V     L     R
C   B E C A U S E
A   U       I
L I G H T N I N G
```
Keyword: HERMIT CRAB

Crossword 2:
```
S U I T C A S E
E     D       I     A
N E E D S     G     S
T     N   W I N G S
E     T     E   A   E
N O I S E     T     M
C     C   T H U M B
E     A       R     L
    S L I P P E R Y
```
Keyword: TIGER PRAWN

Sudokus

1	5	3	6	4	2
2	4	6	1	3	5
4	1	2	5	6	3
3	6	5	4	2	1
5	2	4	3	1	6
6	3	1	2	5	4

4	6	2	1	5	3
3	1	5	4	6	2
2	4	1	5	3	6
5	3	6	2	4	1
1	5	3	6	2	4
6	2	4	3	1	5

2	4	5	1	3	6
1	6	3	4	2	5
6	3	1	2	5	4
4	5	2	6	1	3
5	1	6	3	4	2
3	2	4	5	6	1

Wordsearches

```
d s c a m p i h t f
t a r w c p p e i g
s c a l l o p r g e
h q y f k r s m e o
u u f a v p q i r d
k r i l l p u t p u
a i s i c r i c r c
s t h h f q d r a k
l o b s t e r a w p
y o y s t e r b n o
```

```
r b o c t o p u s e
b n g u a m l w h g
a a h t e b a i r i
r u o s t m a n k i a
n t l e u i d k m n
a l c f s s g c l e t
c l o r i s h r e v c
l e i a e l i a q l a
w d b h p p f l l m
```

Page 58–59

Close up

1 – 4 Acorn barnacle

3 – 5 Striped pyjama squid

5 – 1 Flamingo tongue

2 – 3 Veined octopus

4 – 6 Mimic octopus

6 – 2 Giant triton

Page 60–61

Mazes

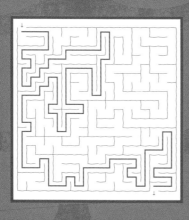

Page 62–63

Guess what?

1. b) Octopus

2. b) 8

3. c) 450 million years

4. a) Flamenco

5. c) Pearl

6. a) Coconut octopus

7. b) Blue

8. a) Their punch can crack the glass

9. c) 7 cm

10. b) 4 metres

Word jumbles

GEODUCK

GHOST CRAB

EMPEROR SHRIMP

OCTOPUS

LOBSTER

Solutions

Crosswords

B	E	D	S		A	L	S	O
E			P		L		M
A	E	R	O	P	L	A	N	E
U		K					L
T	E	L	E	S	C	O	P	E
I			H				T
F	O	R	T	N	I	G	H	T
U		O		N			E
L	A	M	P		A	R	M	S

Keyword: LEATHERBACK

D	E	P	A	R	T		
I		R		A		M		I
S	W	E	E	T	C	O	R	N
T		D			U		T
A	W	A	Y		O	N	C	E
N		T			T		R
C	H	O	C	O	L	A	T	E
E		R		W		I		S
			P	L	A	N	E	T

Keyword: SALTWATER

Page 68-69

Sudokus

4	5	3	2	6	1
1	6	2	3	4	5
5	3	1	6	2	4
2	4	6	1	5	3
6	1	4	5	3	2
3	2	5	4	1	6

4	3	1	6	5	2
2	6	5	1	3	4
3	5	2	4	6	1
1	4	6	5	2	3
5	2	4	3	1	6
6	1	3	2	4	5

3	1	6	2	5	4
4	5	2	3	1	6
2	6	1	4	3	5
5	3	4	6	2	1
1	4	3	5	6	2
6	2	5	1	4	3

Page 70-71

Wordsearches

c	r	o	c	o	d	i	l	e	q
s	g	f	g	p	h	a	o	k	m
h	r	l	a	o	a	s	g	e	r
e	e	a	l	t	w	t	g	d	e
l	e	t	a	t	k	e	e	t	p
l	n	b	p	e	s	r	r	u	i
n	z	a	a	d	b	n	h	r	l
g	d	c	g	r	i	b	e	t	l
o	s	k	o	s	l	o	a	t	e
t	s	s	s	f	l	x	d	e	x

a	n	a	c	o	n	d	a	a	b
a	c	l	o	l	i	v	e	a	e
s	o	i	p	a	n	d	a	a	l
l	r	a	y	s	c	a	l	z	c
i	a	a	t	c	a	v	a	a	h
t	l	k	h	a	a	e	a	k	e
h	r	e	o	l	a	n	n	e	r
e	e	s	n	e	a	o	a	a	s
r	e	a	a	s	a	m	s	r	a
b	f	s	e	a	s	n	a	k	e

100

Spot the difference

Mazes

Guess what?

1. c) 1,500 metres
2. a) The beach
3. a) Hatchlings
4. c) 100–120
5. b) Kemp's Ridley
6. b) 5 metres
7. c) Swim and feed in the ocean
8. a) Yellow-bellied sea snake
9. b) 60
10. c) Ping-pong balls

Word jumbles

HAWKSBILL

SALTWATER

LEATHERBACK

CROCODILE

SEA SNAKE

Solutions

Crosswords

Page 80-81

Keyword: JELLYFISH

Keyword: STARFISH

Sudokus

Page 82-83

2	5	3	1	4	6
4	6	1	2	5	3
6	1	5	3	2	4
3	4	2	6	1	5
5	2	6	4	3	1
1	3	4	5	6	2

1	6	4	2	5	3
2	3	5	1	4	6
3	2	1	5	6	4
4	5	6	3	2	1
6	1	2	4	3	5
5	4	3	6	1	2

5	1	2	3	4	6
6	4	3	2	5	1
3	6	5	1	2	4
1	2	4	6	3	5
4	3	6	5	1	2
2	5	1	4	6	3

Wordsearches

Page 84-85

Page 86–87

Close up

1 – 4 Sunflower star

2 – 6 Staghorn coral

3 – 5 Grooved brain coral

4 – 1 Crown of thorns starfish

5 – 2 Branching vase sponge

6 – 3 Purple-striped jellyfish

Page 88–89

Mazes

 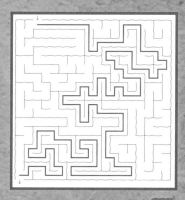

Page 90–91

Guess what?

1. c) Australia

2. a) Clownfish

3. b) 30 metres

4. a) Water gets too warm

5. c) Sunflower star

6. b) Sea slugs

7. c) Every ocean

8. a) Feet

9. b) It grows a new arm

10. b) Sand dollars

Word jumbles

JELLYFISH

SEA CUCUMBER

ANEMONE

CORAL

STARFISH

Look for more puzzle books in this series!

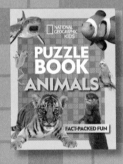